"By living a life based on wisdom and truth, one can discover the divinity of the soul, its union to the universe, the supreme peace and contentment which comes from satisfying the inner drive for self discovery."

—Ancient Egyptian Proverb

The Sketches of 19th Century Egypt

Written

by

Charles Dana Gibson

Published

by

Motmot.org

Copyright

The Sketches of 19th Century Egypt

© 2022 Motmot.org

All rights reserved. No portion of this book may be reproduced without permission from the publisher, except as permitted by copyright law. For permission, please visit the publisher's website at https://motmot.org

Published by Motmot.org

The Biography of Charles Dana Gibson

Charles Dana Gibson, born on July 30, 1867, in Brooklyn Heights, was an American cartoonist who came to prominence during a tremendous social transition in the United States. He is best known for creating the Gibson Girl and "Gibson Man", two charac-ters that became visual icons of that era. An avid student of life, Gibson drew upon the complexity and dynamism he saw around him in everyday life-from cities to farms, from factories and offices to schools and parlors-to create images widely recognized as representative of their time. His satirical daily comic strip The Gumps (1904–1913) displays this range with its diverse characters representing modern New York society: fashionable women, businessmen on horseback rushing home from work at lunchtime, and firefighters rescuing cats from trees.

Later famous for single-panel cartoons published weekly in Life magazine (beginning 1914), he also illustrated numerous books including The Dutch Twins by Lucy Fitch Perkins (1898), A Little Book For Girls And Boys by Selina Davenport Gibbons (1900), Teddy Bears At Home by Edith Hurd Woodbury (1903) and Fairy Tales Of Childhood byCharles Perrault & Gustave Doré (1920).

Egypt in the Late 19th Century

In the 19th century, Egypt The Ottoman Empire occupied Egypt. Khedive Ismail, a vassal to the Ottoman Sultan, ruled the country just a few decades before Charles Dana Gibson's visit, so the Turkish influence was enormous for Egypt during the 19th and early 20th centuries.

It was a dark period in Egypt's history when it was in a weak and dependent state. Egypt's massive debt from the construction of the Suez Canal, which French contractors and engineers constructed, also left Egypt in poverty and bankruptcy. Egypt had to borrow money from European countries to pay for the construction, and the debt grew.

The Egyptians had to face a period of significant political turbulence. Khedive Ismail was accused of mismanagement and was forced to pay for the Canal's construction. This resulted in the bankruptcy of the Egyptian government. The rebellion against the Khedive led to the British occupation of Egypt in 1882.

This occupation lasted until 1952. The British occupation was characterized by the strengthening of the British Empire, the control of Egypt's finances, and the modernization of the Egyptian economy. The British extended the Suez canal and railway systems and built more dams. The economic development of this period helped the country become one of the world's most important cotton and rice producers.

When Egypt became a British colony, the British government decided to remove non-British investors from the country, especially the French, who had helped build the Suez Canal.

The French were forced to leave Egypt, and the British took control of the Suez Canal.

14

Life in 19th Century Egypt

After the fall of Egypt to the British, the socioeconomic and political foundations of the modern Egyptian state were set. The transformation of Egypt into a capitalist economy began in the late 19th century when the country started to export raw materials to Europe and import manufactured goods. This trend continued into the 20th century, resulting in Egypt becoming increasingly integrated into the world capitalist system. The transformation of Egypt led to the emergence of a ruling elite composed of large landowners of Turco-Circassian origin and the creation of a class of medium-sized landowners of Egyptian origin who played an increasingly important role in the political and economic life of the country. In the countryside, peasants were dispossessed because of debt, and many landless peasants migrated to the cities, where they joined the swelling ranks of the unemployed. In the towns, a professional middle class emerged composed of civil servants, lawyers, teachers, and technicians. Finally, Western ideas and cultural forms were introduced into the country. The modernization of Egypt was achieved through a process of conquest and colonization.

A new class of large landowners emerged in Egypt during the latter half of the nineteenth century. These landowners were virtually independent of the central government. They were allowed to keep local order and administer justice for a share of the taxes they collected. To strengthen the state's authority, the rulers of Egypt tried to tie the peasants to the land by requiring them to pay a fixed share of their crops to the landowner. The main target of the drive to tie the peasants to the land was fellahin or native Egyptians. Although fellahin were exempted from military service, they were required to pay taxes.

Approximately 2 million out of the 10 million people in Egypt lived in towns and cities at the turn of the century. Out of those 2 million, 500,000 lived in cities with a population of more than 20,000. The population of Alexandria grew as it became the financial and commercial center for the cotton industry. The increase in Egypt's urban population was primarily due to peasants migrating from the countryside. Many became workers or petty traders, but most joined the ranks of the unemployed. By the turn of the century, a working class had emerged. It was made up mostly of transport and building workers and workers in industries that had been established--sugar refineries, ginning mills, and cigarette factories. But a large part of the new urban lower class were people without fixed employment. Life for the average Egyptians was harsh; well-paying jobs were scarce. The traditional middle class began to decline in status and wealth. Income inequality increased as the Suez Canal brought untold riches to a select few.

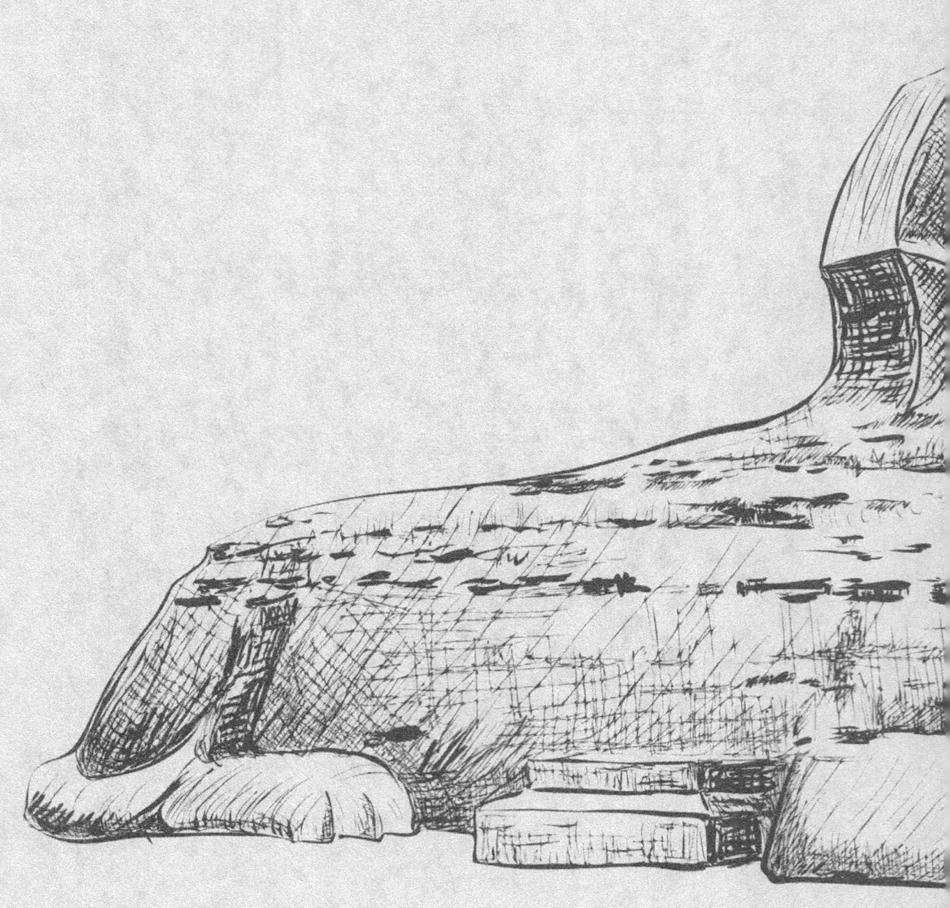

SKETCHES IN EGYPT
BY
C. D GIBSON

FIRST CHAPTER

A Son of the Desert.

Egypt has sat for her likeness longer than any other country. Nothing disturbs her composure. Financial ruin may stare her in the face, and armies may come and go, but each year the Nile rises and spreads out over her, and all traces of disturbances are gone.

Newspapers may be busy telling of her troubles, but very few of those troubles seem to affect her expression. The stockholders in London worry and send out more Englishmen to look after their interests. Sugar factories are inspected, and the barrage is doctored. But it is all very quietly done.

The French cabinet may resign because of her, and the English may increase their armies for her sake, but she shows few signs of these compliments. All is tranquil. The only disturbance seems to be made by the dragomans who meet you at the station.

A Peddler.

Important events follow each other so closely in Egypt that a year-old guidebook is several chapters too short. Last year it was Kitchener's campaign against the dervishes, and now the French threaten to interfere with England's march to the Cape. The dragoman is sometimes as satisfactory as the guidebook, and it is often pleasant to find how soon he is through with his recitation, and you are allowed to go alone among the great temples. Earthquakes have shaken some in orderly ruin as if the unseen hands of the men who built them were quietly and slowly building them up again.

But there is a temptation to grow sentimental over Egypt. It is far more cheerful than it sounds. It is a happy place for a holiday—a country where I can sketch. I drew these sketches between December 1897 and March 1898. I have been asked to help them tell their story of that part of Egypt the tourist is most likely to see, where the old and the new world meet most often.

The ancient Egyptian artist must have been thrilled. Temples were built with great smooth walls for him to cover with pictures that required very little writing to go with them, seldom more than Pharaoh's cartouches, and even these he made more like a picture than a name. That must have been very pleasant, and it should have compensated him for all the restrictions imposed upon him by the high priest of those days, who often limited his choice of subject to a king. The choice of topic is now unlimited. There have never been so many different kinds of people in Egypt before. But it would be difficult to draw the king directly, for there are many differences of opinion as to who he is.

I left New York with a small library of Egyptian guidebooks, and in nearly every one of them was a good description of a traveler's feelings upon arriving at Alexandria or Port Saïd.

24

I have been in both places, and about the same sensations will fit either port, and traveling is too personal a matter to describe at length unless it is done with skill.

The Slipper Bazaar, Cairo, January 22, 1898.

To give advice is much more straightforward, and mine is that if you are on a steamer going through the Canal, don't stay on her until she gets to Ismailia, but disembark at Port Saïd and get to Cairo that night by rail. You will see as much of the Canal as you want to, and you will not run the chance of being delayed a day, as the *Königin Luise* was last year by a little tramp steamer that had run foul of a coal barge.

A Dealer in Antiquities.

More advice is to look out of the right-hand window of the car for a first glimpse of the pyramids, the first sure proof that you are in Napoleon's Egypt. After they are once found, it is easy for your eye to follow them through palm trees and over mud villages until darkness interferes. Then you come to the station in Cairo, a hotbed of porters and dragomans, and through the confusion, you finally reach Shepheard's, on the street like a great show window—all but the plate glass—full of odds and ends from all the world. The dragomans and porters hand in new arrivals. It is as if you climbed over the footlights to assist in the performance. You finally stand before the good-looking Mr. Bailer at the back of the stage. You will get it if he thinks you will stand in a room overlooking the stable yard. The following day I moved to the sunny side, overlooking the garden, where a tame pelican walked among tall palm trees.

Egyptian High Life.

26

The Present Situation.

The dragoman who first lays hands on you claims you for his own. You will find him waiting for you in the morning.

A Village on the Road to the Pyramids.

He will sell you antiques, will take you snipe-shooting. He

knows when the dervishes will howl or whirl or where there is a native wedding, to which he will take you. It may be Shepheard's fame or Egypt's magic name, but it all has a beautiful charm.

In the Fish-Market.

The remains of Rameses and Seti lie on their backs out in the Giza Museum, and there is a strong desire to hurry to them, even though they will keep them. But the panorama in front of Shepheard's is absorbing, and your first morning will most likely be spent watching it.

My first afternoon was spent with an evil-eyed dragoman whose pockets were filled with dirty cards and letters, all testimonials from former customers proving

The Bridge.

28

that he was, as he continually told me, the best dragoman in the business. He could recite some of "Mother Goose" but knew very little English. With him, I drove through streets that might have been in Paris and by barracks and sentries that might have been in London to a river that could only be in Egypt.

My carriage went between two bronze lions and joined in the procession of camels across the bridge over the famous river to the Giza side, where tall trees meet overhead. Then to a smaller bridge, more trees, quaint shipping, and a stucco palace, once a harem where some of Ismail's wives lived.

Rameses the Great.

Then a museum, the temporary resting-place of those uneasy mummied heads that once wore Egypt's crown; miniature mouse-colored donkeys on all sides, and, streaking in among them, tall camels; then seven more miles of trees and a good causeway to the pyramids. Since then, I have gone over the road many times, and I believe that the Nile valley would make an ideal "happy hunting ground," to which all good tourists might go when cruel waves have ceased to toss them, and their hotel lives are over.

At Lady Grenfell's Masquerade Ball—on the eve of Kitchener's departure for the Soudan.

All too soon, you must go back to Cairo, where the Bedouin ceases to be the proud son of the desert and becomes a peddler, where sheep become mutton and clover is only fod-

A Descendant of the Prophet—El Saied Ahmad Abdel Khalek Affandi, Sheik el Sadat.

der. But Cairo is about what the tourist wants and what the hotel proprietor thinks the tourist wants. He fills the halls of his hotel with gaily painted columns, and on each side of the staircase are gaudy figures; for those tourists who take their Egypt between the slipper bazaar and the fish market.

The Giza side of the river is more restful, with its ferry to Bulak, its gardens, and its khedival sporting club, which is Egypt as England would have it— polo twice a week, croquet and rackets, a grandstand, and a steeplechase course. The same men who play polo spend their mornings in the desert, teaching their troops to form hollow squares against the day they will have to meet the dervishes.

You should choose your own Cairo. If you leave it to a dragoman, you will get mostly howling dervishes and mosques; and if you leave it to a donkey boy, there is no tell-

A Bargain in the Ghezireh Gardens.

31

ing where he will take you—most likely to the fish market. But with a guidebook and a bicycle, you will miss very little that lies between the citadel and the pyramids.

A Dancing-Girl.

Cairo is not all hotel life, and bazaars lining narrow streets like open fireplaces, filled with putty-faced Turks as watchful as the brown buzzards that fly overhead.

Some streets are difficult to find, leading to forgotten courtyards with great trees standing in the middle, latticed windows bulging out over uneven pavements below, where black and gray crows roam. In such a place sits the neglected Sheik el Sadat, a lineal descendant of the prophet.

Through a doorway, in one corner of a tiled room, stands the gold-mounted saddle on which his ancestors once proudly rode. That was long before the days of the Suez Canal, boulevards, stucco palaces, and the opera house. At court, the sheik is no longer the fashion, but a little band of Mohammed followers still believe in him. To them, the sheik and his old house are sacred. Through the thirty days of Ramadan, they sat and howled in his courtyard and respectfully kissed his hand; and, like the sheik, there

A Daughter of the Nile.

must be many other distinguished Oriental relics of the days gone by, left behind by the former tenants, and of no use to the present occupants.

In Egypt, the English hold the reins; one of these days, the Egyptian donkey may turn to the left when you meet it, as its distant relative in Whitechapel does. The donkey stays to the right and staggers along under a load too big for it. Today it is not the fashion in Cairo. The donkey is only ridden by tourists after dark, through narrow, crooked streets for a carriage. But up the river, it is very different. There you learn to like it.

From its back, you first see Karnak and the statues of Memnon, and it is forever associated in your memory with the tombs of the kings. Tourists quarrel over it; in most cases, its name is "Rameses, the Great." Its chief complaint must be that an Englishman weighs more than an Egyptian, but it should consider how much better off the Egyptian is since the English have held the reins.

On the Road to Cairo.

The donkey will only know of this through observation and from the words of the English tourists. It will never get it from a Frenchman, and the Egyptian, who could tell him, is sulky and stupidly wishes that he had been rescued by someone else.

The mixed-race Jew and Turk in the "Mooskee" is too busy; all the rest of Egypt doesn't know why they are better off or who to thank for law and order or the improved irrigation that gives them a fair chance with the rest of civilized humanity. But whether the donkey knows it or not, it is much hotter off, for an Englishman never rides it when it is old and weak, and that is more than it can expect from its Egyptian friends, who often ride it two at a time.

At Shepheard's, people put aside their guidebooks for a while. It is a play that requires no libretto. On the crowded piazza overlooking the street, London shopkeepers and foreign noblemen elbow each other, and all celebrities look very alike.

Cairo is the foyer of Egypt. Going to Egypt and not going up the Nile is very much like standing outside of a theater and watching the audience go in, and then waiting until they come out, to glean some idea of the play from their conversation. But the tourists who go up the river see the drama of Egypt with all its fantastic scenery, feeling far superior to those who waited for them at Shepheard's. After one month on the river, it is with a very different feeling they come back to the museum at Giza and look at the face of Seti and his distinguished son, whom they have tracked from Sakkara to Philæ and back to their tombs, where they had hoped to rest in peace, surrounded by all that a first-class mummy requires.

34

*Our Bisharin
Friends, Assuan.*

SECOND CHAPTER

Some Egypt-bound tourists decide to go up the Nile before they buy their tickets at the company's office in Bowling Green. If they are good sailors, others make up their minds before reaching Naples. Some are ill all the way to Port Saïd and don't cave. But most travelers are sure to decide one way or the other soon after Mount Etna has been left behind, for the East begins for most people from that moment. If the guidebooks fail to persuade you, there is pretty sure to be a fellow passenger who will. The man who once saw Upper Egypt does his best to make you dissatisfied with Lower Egypt. He can easily show you that your journey's end is not Cairo but, at the very least, the first cataract. This is the shortest distance he will listen to. And after he has your promise to go that far, he tells you of the wonders that can only be seen by going on to the second cataract.

My fellow passenger was an old traveler. Others besides myself fell under the spell of his eloquence; before we had been at Shepheard's a week, we were a party of six, with the steam-dahabiyeh *Nitocris* chartered for a month, beginning December 12. There were growing plants, rugs, a piano on her deck, and six staterooms below. Salem Ghesiri was our dragoman. He spoke good English and knew the river by heart. Before we left, we spent a few days buying cork hats and sun umbrellas.

Our Christmas Dinner, Esneh, December 23.

By ten o'clock on the morning of the 12th, the crew had unloaded the trucks that had brought our belongings down from Shepheard's, and we had started with the wind and the current so strong against us that it was all we could do to make six miles an hour against them.

On our left were the mud houses of Old Cairo, with ancient quarries in the distance, and on the right, far beyond a forest of slanting masts that belonged to the picturesque ships which lined the bank, were the tops of the pyramids that we were leaving for a month. As evening approached, the right bank seemed peopled with silhouettes of camels, donkeys, and men, while the figures on the opposite bank were rose-color. To us, the day was excellent, but to the crew, it must have been cold, for their heads were wrapped in shawls, and they huddled together in groups about the deck. The awning over us had been removed, and Ali, the pilot, looked like a partly unwrapped mummy as he sat at the wheel.

Those who go up the river in a dahabiyeh like to feel that

they are in the same boat as the travelers whose books they read from New York to Port Saïd. This would be an enjoyable feeling if it did not suggest the responsibility of keeping a record of days that, from all accounts, are sure to be of so much importance.

There is a sentimental belief that each day on the river is of the greatest importance, just as if thousands of tourists on Cook's steamers were not taking the same journey each year. So overpowering becomes this delusion that even letters home seem to take the form of historical biographies and sound like messages that are sometimes found floating in bottles thrown overboard by shipwrecked people.

Karnak, January 2, 1898.

The Nile seems to insist that all mention of it should be made in the form of a diary, for, with very few exceptions, all accounts adopt that mode of expression when they come to it. Cairo and Upper Egypt may be treated in the form of essays. Still, the endless parallel banks of the river immediately suggest that all days will be very much alike and lose their

40

identity unless they are numbered and described.

It seems to be of the most significant importance to find the best way to spell the name of the mud village where you tie up for the night (which name most of the guidebooks spell differently)—as if it made any difference to the people at home.

A Karnak Beggar.

Salem Ghesiri Dragoman.

But the diaries on the *Nitocris* during that month were very conscientious and particular about these small things, and I think they will all agree on their spelling, for each one of us waited until all the others had decided upon the most popular way to spell the names of these various landmarks before we wrote them down.

We soon made friends with our crew. There were sixteen of them. They were from every part of Egypt and of all colors, shading from the engineer, who was a cream-colored Turk—when his face was washed—to Ali, who must have been a Sudanese.

Our head steward was almost as black, and the second steward was another of the cream-colored variety. We seldom saw the Cook. Sometimes he would

All, the Pilot.

41

put his head and shoulders out of the hatchway, with his arms on the deck, and then we could see that he was a tiny, white-faced Turk with a large black mustache.

Statue of Thothmes,
Karnak.

Lunching in Karnak.

Salem was a Syrian Christian and had lost all his earnings in an unprofitable exhibit at the World's Fair in Chicago. His costumes were always elaborate and ornamental, with his silk sashes and fancy turbans. He superintended our meals and suggested the next day's program during dinner so we would read Charles Dudley Warner's and Miss Edwards's opinions of our next stopping-place with our coffee.

After our first dinner, we tied to the bank, by a little village, Salem said, just big enough to have a name. It was dark, and we could hear and see nothing, so we took his word for it.

An Assiût Donkey.

We were off early the following day, and the river's banks were fringed with sugar cane and sakiehs all that day. The many boats we passed were loaded with natives, sometimes perched upon loads of grain or mixed in with turkeys and cattle.

On December 14, we made our first landing and had our first donkey ride at Beni-Hassan, one hundred and seventy-one miles from Cairo. The Egyptian police officers who accompanied us to the tombs were out of keeping with the peaceful look of the place and only succeeded in keeping at a distance the children, who were very pretty.

From the cliffs back of the village, we had our first view of the valley of the Nile, with its delicate green fields, beginning immediately at the foot of the sun-baked hills on which we stood. I rode back before the rest to make a sketch, but the arrival of the post-boat put an end to that, and its passengers soon had our donkeys, beggars, naked children, police officers, and all, and were taking them back

Tombs of the Kings, Thebes.

to the tombs we had just left. The post-boat was to us what the footprints in the sand must have been to Robinson Crusoe. Our frame of mind changed. We finally reconciled to the fact that we were not doing anything uncommon, and from that moment, our diaries suffered. Then the most contagious of all Nile ambitions seized us, and our one desire was to find a mummy.

Most of the 15th was spent with Baedeker, preparing for Assiût, where we were to tie up for the night.

After an early breakfast, we climbed the bank and found that beggars chiefly inhabited it. We visited the tombs and re-

44

turned to the dahabiyeh by the bazaars, where
the natives were dyeing the dark-blue cloth they
all dressed in. That afternoon we came upon an
army of pelicans on a mud flat in the middle
of the river. They got up at the sound of our
whistle, and we lost them far ahead in the twi-
light, and we thought of that tame pelican that
waddles about in Shepheard's stable yard.

*A Guardian
of the Tem-
ple.*

The next day we went by mud villages at the
foot of high mountains of white limestone un-
til we stopped at Farshut for coal and tried to awaken some
sign of friendliness in the natives, who were as dull as the
mud banks on which they sat.

"Most of the day was spent with Baedeker."

On the afternoon of the 18th, we reached Keneh, and in
fifteen minutes, we were on donkeys, going by villages filled
with children and barking dogs, on our way to the temple of
Dendera. This was our first big temple, and Salem had made

45

it his chief excuse for hurrying us away from Beni-Hassan, Assiût, and the rest. Our donkeys raced along the edge of an empty canal, through herds of goats and buffalo, until we saw a low pile of stones in the distance, and then we reached the half-buried temple and lighted candles and went down into it and looked up at the mighty columns. Salem repeated all that the guidebooks knew and then took us around to the back wall and showed us the famous likeness of Cleopatra and her son Cæsarion.

Salem was pleased with how we took our first temple and rewarded us by saying it was only the beginning of what was to come. We complimented him on his choice of subjects, blew out our candles, picked the candle grease from our fingers, and reached the dahabiyeh by sundown.

Christmas, 1897.

By one o'clock on December 19, we were abreast of the promised Karnak and could see the top of its towers and obelisk. We had saved most of our enthusiasm for this place,

46

and we were anxious to get ashore and expend it; reluctantly, we went by it a few miles to Luxor for a better landing, where a bank-load of natives watched us until four o'clock. Then we walked through them to the village and temple of Luxor, which served as a curtain-raiser to the next day's visit to the greatest of all temples.

Guardians of the Temple.

That evening a Cook's steamer arrived, and the crowd deserted us on the bank. After dinner, Ghesiri entertained the sheiks of the donkey boys and made arrangements for our mounts for the next day. Two of us volunteered to go to the village and locate the dancing that the guidebooks said could be found here, but we learned there would be none until the following Saturday.

The next day was spent at Karnak, where Ghesiri led us over its famous stones until lunch was brought from the *Nitocris* and served in a colonnade surrounded by columns resembling giant granite lozenges, piled at all angles, one on top of the other, like ancient friends, those who had fought successfully with time supporting those who had been less fortunate; and apart from the rest, requiring no support, and with no friends to be helped, stood the greatest column of them all, the lonely survivor of the great peristyle court, with its lotus capital, looking down on all but its lonely rival, an obelisk. It seems as though it had been polished and placed there the day before, in striking contrast to its unfortunate mate, which centuries ago gave up battling with earthquakes and wars, and now lies, a hopeless ruin, at its feet.

We spent the next three days at Karnak and Thebes, saving the tombs of the kings until we should stop again on our way down from Assuan.

And now the critical question was, Where should we spend Christmas? The better we knew Karnak and Thebes, the more forbidding they had grown. They were too stiff and formal, and their great rigid Rameses too depressing for a Christmas. We wanted a cheerful temple, and we found it at Komombos.

Christmas Night—"Auld Lang Syne."

We left Karnak on the morning of December 24 and spent Christmas eve at Edfu. That night the deck was entirely housed in canvas. The crew sat in a circle back of the smoke stack, and while they divided the cigarettes we had bought for them at Luxor, they listened to our "Down upon the Su-

48

wanee River."

We came on deck on Christmas morning and found that Ghesiri had transformed it into a bower of palm branches, sugar cane, and oranges. The crew was all smiles, and when we presented them with the price of a sheep, they gave us three cheers and a merry Christmas. More cigarettes were distributed, and shortly after breakfast, we started for Komombos.

Thebes, January 2, 1898.

There was little in the day to remind a New Englander of Christmas. We sat by the deck in the lightest clothes and watched village after village. It was good to see our old friends, the water wheels, and cheerful sakiehs again, who looked better to us after our somber stay at Karnak. Early in the afternoon, we came to Komombos, the temple we were looking for, and tied to the river's bank just below it; and if you must be traveling on Christmas, there can be no better place to stop.

At Komombos, the never-resting Nile has worked its way to

the foot of the little hill on which the temple is making its last stand against time. Some kind friends have covered the bank with stones, but the river is slowly wearing them away, and sooner or later, it will claim its own. It will be a pity, for Komombos's temple is dainty compared to Karnak, where great stiff Rameses stand with their arms folded across their breasts in very much the same manner as the real arms are held in the glass case at the Giza Museum.

Home Visitors.

At Karnak, there were miles of half-buried walls, cut deep in them gigantic figures of Rameses, with one hand raised about to strike off the heads of enemies done up in bundles like asparagus held by the hair of their heads, while armies are shown flying in confusion. The bas-reliefs at Komombos are more cheerful and cut with more extraordinary skill. They represent the ancient gods of Egypt in their more playful moods, floating down the Nile, spearing miniature hippopotamuses and crocodiles, with here and there a triumphant procession.

50

The debris of the forgotten city that once covered Komombos has been removed, and the great hall, with its holy of holies now exposed to the light of day, is swept by the wind as clean as a Dutch kitchen; and yet the carvings are as fresh as the day they were made. From the *Nitocris* to the temple is only a few steps through some sugar cane. It was a novel experience to find no donkey boys with their patient and sleepy donkeys.

But the natives differed from any we had previously seen and proved that we were getting into real Africa. They were primarily Nubians and very black, our preconceived idea of what an African should be.

Komombos and Philæ are the only temples we climbed up to, and it seems to me that they, above all others, lend themselves more readily to the sentimental tourist. It is easier for the imagination to people them; they are more like dwellings.

After tea had been brought from the *Nitocris* and served in its portals, we all decided that Komombos would be the temple to own. That evening the crew hung lanterns around the deck among the sugar canes and palms, and after dinner, they gave an exhibition, which started well enough with a dance by the first mate.

Since then, I have found that all travelers on the Nile are likely to have this same experience. We were proof against the "Dhabir Devil" that the guidebooks had warned us against, but Baedeker had made no mention of the possibility of this entertainment happening to us; still, the crew went at it as though it was an old story with them, and as I write this there may be some unsuspecting tourist about to go through with it. It sounds very good-natured on the part of the crew, and if the entertainment had stopped when the mate had finished the dance, it would have been well enough, but the dance was only to hold our attention while the others were getting ready and then the dreary horse-play began.

There was a barber shop scene in which flour paste was used, and a door-mat acted as a towel. A crew that mutinies are tame compared with an Egyptian crew that acts. We stopped them as soon as possible without hurting their feelings, and they subsided and formed a circle back of the smoke stack. We spent the rest of the evening playind cards, and by mid-night all was still but the river, which never rests.

The port.

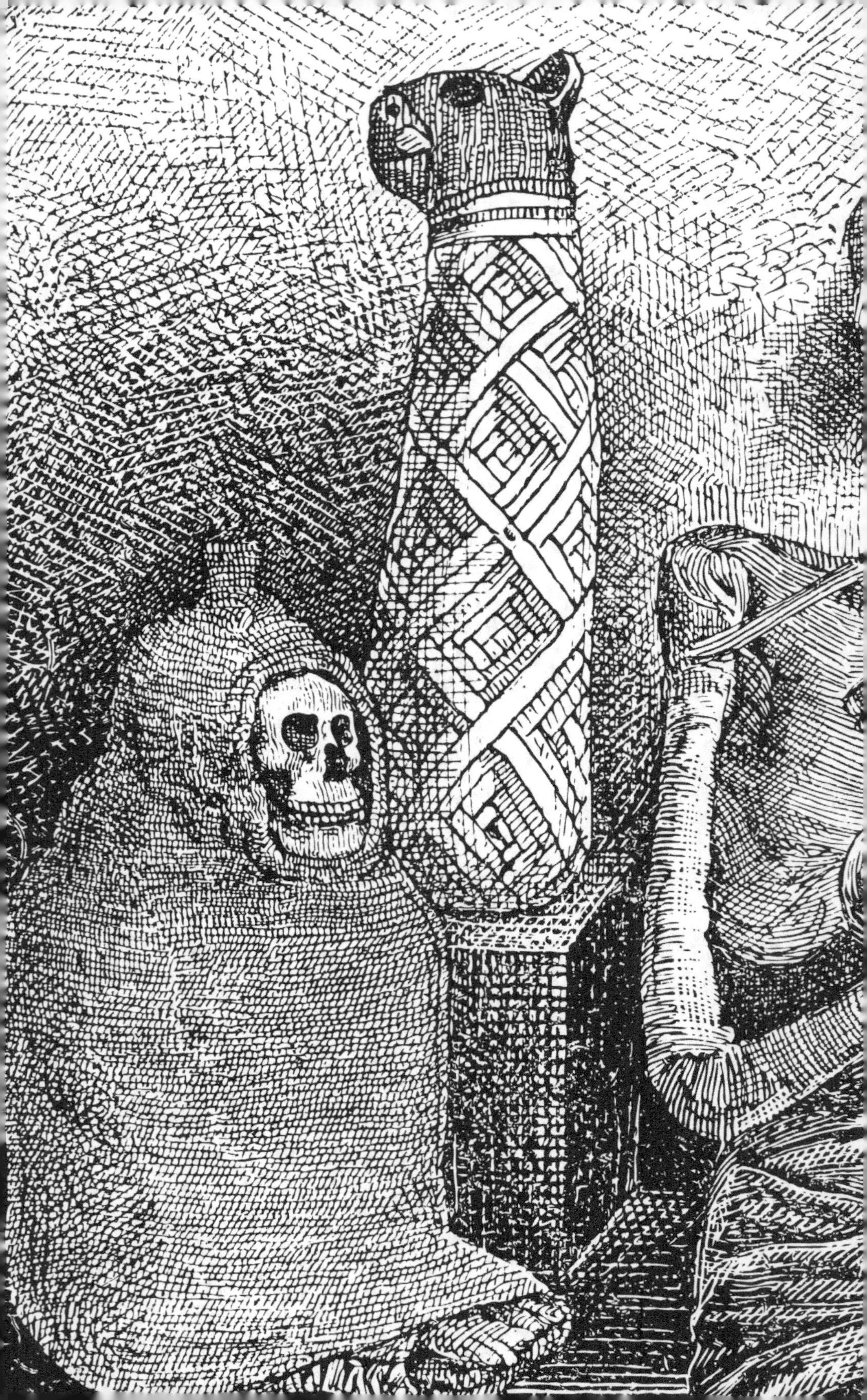

THIRD CHAPTER

The starting of the engines had us up reasonably early the following day, and we found the country very much changed. The desert now came to the river's edge, and granite had taken the place of limestone; it seemed as though we had come to the end of fertile Egypt. Two white vultures were the only living things in sight. Then we went to some beautiful bends in the river, and the sakiehs once more began to dip up the muddy water, but the skins of the men who worked them had changed: they glistened like coal in the sunlight.

On the Bank.

By two o'clock, we reached Aswan and moored to the island of Elephantine, just opposite the town, from which any number of little bright-painted ferry-boats rowed toward us.

After a few minutes, some thin-legged Egyptian policemen and a few natives were on the bank, and a small boy with a stick had been selected to mind the turkeys we had brought from Esneh. Some of the poor birds were very weak on their legs, and where they ought to have been red, they were only a pale salmon color; but the little Cook promised they would be all right in a day or two. Some crew had homes on the island; they all wore their best clothes and were met by friends. They immediately established a laundry on shore, and an oven building proved that we would be there for some time.

His Highness Prince Mahomet Ali, Cairo, February 14, 1898.

We began the 27th with a visit to the tombs on Grenfell Hill, high on the river's bank, below Elephantine. There was a strong wind, full of sand, from the south, and the light natives had trouble getting the heavy boat to the foot of the hill. The wind helped us back to the *Nitocris*, and after lunch, we crossed the river to Assuan, where the inhabitants seemed especially prepared for tourists. The natives were more theatrical in Assuan, and the bazaars were filled with musical instruments, made as primitive as possible to please the traveler.

Shopping.

There is a railroad at Assuan. It is only a tiny, disconnected link, but someday it will be part of a road to the Cape, vestibule trains will run over it, and passengers may get only glimpses of Philæ from car windows. Think of being on a train that went by Pharaoh's Bed in the night! But it is impossible to believe that the world could become used to such a wonderful place, and it is to be hoped that all trains will go slow when they come to Philæ; for without it, Egypt would be like "Romeo and Juliet" without a balcony. It is the most romantic ruin in Egypt and marks the end of the first-cataract tourist's journey.

If the *Nitocris* had been a sailing-dahabiyeh and had belonged

to us, and if the season had been younger and the river high-
er, we would have had her pulled up one cataract after another until we had made some crucial discoveries. Still, we were
one-month tourists on a hired boat, and that night, while the
Nitocris was tied fast to some large wooden pegs driven deep
into the beach, we read how the *Rip Van Winkle* and other
dahabiyehs had gone to Abu-Simbel.

Shepheard's Hotel, Cairo.

The following day we chose the nine-o'clock train, in pref-
erence to camels and donkeys. After some minutes of rock-
ing and twisting in the little box car, we were ferried from
the mainland to the famous island, where we were to forget
Komombos and all the others amid new beauties, which no
guidebook can exaggerate.

After lunch, we walked to the island's northern end, hoarded a big, clumsy, eight-oared boat with a great deal of rigging lashed overhead, and our homeward journey began. There was a crew of ten, and we soon had the greatest respect for their skill, especially one little man with crooked teeth, who sat in the stern and shouted over our heads at the men in the boat.

*A Luxor Danc-
ing-girl.*

The rapids were tame enough at first. The wind was strong against us, and we found some shelter behind the high granite islands we drifted among. The river had worn them into fan-tastic shapes so closely resembling temples that hieroglyphics had been cut on the polished stones by the Pharaohs, who never tired of seeing their names in print.

At one place, we stopped and watched ten or fifteen boys swim and float down a part of the rapids. They would come shivering up to us, and the next instant, they would be in the water shoot-ing by us on a log, screaming to attract our attention, and then back again to us, with their teeth chattering for bakshish.

But after that, it was very different. The man at the tiller

60

The Sheik of the Pyramids.

half stood up, and I could see, by the little patches of sand on his forehead, that the wrinkles there had formed in two parallel lines, that he had been praying while we had been watching the boys swim, and by the same sign I could see that most of the crew had been doing the same thing.

Mohammed must have been with us, for fifty times within half that number of minutes we needed help. With the little man in the stern continually wetting his lips and jamming the tiller from side to side, apparently steering in just the wrong place, and always proving that he was right, we "shot" over the uneven surface of the river, dodging half-buried rocks, first near one bank and then the other, until we reached the natural bed of the river.

Camel-back.

Here the crew began their battle with the wind, and by evening, after much chanting and hard rowing on their part, we

61

reached the *Nitocris*, feeling very much as if our faces had been sandpapered. We made friends with four little Bisharin girls during our stay at Elephantine.

On Grenfell Hill. The Keeper of the Tomb, Assuan, December 29, 1897.

They were graceful and pretty and had the power to make the most dismal tomb cheerful. They followed us to the quarries back of Aswan, turned the top of the half-finished obelisk into a stage, and danced in the sunlight while the blackest man in Africa played an instrument of his invention. And the last I remember of Aswan is their four little figures wrapped in the brightest-colored shawls that anyone could buy in Lower Egypt, and they waved their hands until a bend in the river hid them.

62

It was a novelty to find ourselves going with the current, which had been until now against us, and we could count on much bigger runs; but there was double the danger of running on a sand-bar, and from that time on, there was always a man with a pole in the bow.

At the Races, Khedival Sporting Club.

On the 30th, we stopped beneath our old friend Komombos and visited Edfu the next day; and from the top of its towers, we looked into the mud-walled yards of the town, where little fly-covered children stopped playing with goats and called to us, even at that height, for bakshish.

On the 31st, we were once more in Luxor, where the donkey boys and beggars gave us a hearty welcome. Again we visited Thebes and were followed from tomb to tomb by the usual vendors of imitation antiques and shriveled mummy hands.

Our trips back from Thebes were always animated by donkey races across the great fields of young wheat, in the middle of which the great Memnons sit. Those races generally proved that "Columbus" was a faster donkey than "New York."

An Assuan Beggar.

Pharaoh must have continually thought of the future. His tombs at Thebes show how anxious he was to outlast time. And it seems complicated that his carefully prepared plans should have been interfered with. How impressive it would be to find the king whose one wish was to lie at the end of the long underground passage. He must have visited it often before his death. He might have superintended its building and criticized the drawings that decorate its walls. But the sarcophagus is now empty, and its lid is broken, and the king's new friends have put him in a cheap wooden house; written on a piece of cardboard, and tacked on the glass case in which he now lies, is the name he was so fond of cutting in granite.

One year more or less makes very little difference to Egypt, but the New Year was welcomed adequately aboard the *Nitocris*, for one of us had never seen a January 1 before. So it happened that, even in Egypt, the occasion was treated as a novelty. The *Nitocris* blossomed out with lanterns and looked as well that night as her more graceful rivals, the sailing-dahabiyehs, that were anchored above and below us.

January 4 was our last day at Luxor. We had ridden up the limestone valley at Thebes to the kings' tombs and spent several days and a moonlight night at Karnak. We had said good-bye to our donkey boys. Mine had held an umbrella over me with one hand and had fought natives at the same time with the other, and I hope that someday he will be a dragoman. Before daylight on the 5th, we had once more started north, with only five more days left on the river. We tied to the bank at night, walked through moonlighted villages, and did our best to imagine that our journey had only just begun.

An Artist in the Mouskie.

On the evening of the 7th, an extraordinary thing happened. It rained hard enough to make a noise on the awning over us, and in the excitement, we almost forgot that there were only three more days between Cairo and us. We had begun to count the hours and to dread that fatal bend in the river that would show us the pyramids at Sakkara, where we were to spend our last night. We passed dahabiyehs with American and English flags flying over them, and we were filled with envy.

Handkerchiefs and parasols were sympathetically waved at us. We may have looked cheerful at a distance, but it was a forlorn, childish feeling to be taken home because our time was up, and our dahabiyeh had another engagement. We felt that all the other boats knew our secret, and we even suspected the crew of having become tired of us and only remaining civil to collect the present they were expecting.

Beni-Hassan.

Ghesiri's suggestion that we spend the night of the 10th at Cairo proved they were anxious to do with us. Still, we did not incline to be tied to the bank at Cairo overnight, waiting to be sent away in the morning before a crowd of natives and possibly others who had chartered our boat. We would stay

66

at Sakkara and not get to Cairo one minute before our time was up.

On the 8th, we visited a sugar factory at Tel-el-Amarna, and later on, the same day passed our first landing place, Beni-Hassan.

By noon on the 9th, we reached the fatal bend in the river and saw that we were once more in the land of pyramids, and we were soon tied to the bank beneath which once stood the city of Memphis.

At Philæ.

We rode to Marietta's House, past the pyramids and the colossal Rameses lying on his back among tall palms, surrounded, for some reason, by a mud house, as if the great granite figure had not already proved that it could continue its battle with time unassisted by a few mud bricks and some tin roofing that is very much in the way.

We lighted candles, walked through the mausoleum's hot, suffocating galleries, and peered into the vast granite sarcophagi that once held the mummied sacred bulls. Then we rode to the tomb of Ti, and Ghesiri's last lecture was about that gentleman.

In the distance was Cairo; even a view of the pyramids at Giza and the citadel failed to console us, and we still mourned our late month on the Nile. We took our last donkey ride through the palms that now grow where Memphis once stood and reached the *Nitocris* by sundown.

"As good an imitation of Monte Carlo as the law allows."

By midday on the 10th, we shook hands with the crew and left the *Nitocris* tied to the bank where we had first found her, just as though nothing had happened; and, after all, what had happened was this: six more tourists had gone to the first cataract and back, and a few more Egyptian sketches had been made.

For us, the performance of the Nile was at an end, and we were once more in the streets on our way to the Ghezireh

Hotel, with a determination to console ourselves with Cairo, which now looked to us, after our stay in the country, like a full-grown European capital.

"The man who has 'been there before.'"

By January 10, the season had commenced, and the prices of rooms had doubled. Since we left, several steamers from the west had brought an army of tourists, who were turning Africa into New York, London, and Paris. And at the Casino, in the Ghezireh Gardens, was as good an imitation of Monte Carlo as the law allows, but such a poor one that even the Frenchmen who worked it seemed ashamed of themselves, and the New Yorker who owned it was very seldom seen there.

At Shepheard's, there is always the man who has "been there before," Like the same man at the play. He sits beside you

and interprets the picture. You finally promise that you will
not go to the *monskie* without him and that you will not see
the Sphinx by moonlight unless he is there; for if you do, not
having been there before, you will be sure to go too early or
too late.

In a Coffee-house, Cairo.

He says the moon should be at just such an angle and no
other. The peddlers in the monskie know him, and while they
entertain him with little cups of sweet tea, they complain that
they have had no luck since they last saw him. They ask eager-
ly after that gentleman he brought to them the year before—
the gentleman who had such exquisite taste and backed it
up so generous with his money. And you drink their tea and
feel, as you leave the shops, after having only looked at their
things, that they will never ask affectionately after you.

The man who has been there before generally walks in front

70

of you as if he were not as anxious to have you see the place as he is to have you see that he knows his way about; and, after all, it is no small thing to be proud of. If I ever go to the mouskie again, I shall pity the greenhorn with me.

At Komombos.

The bazaars are dirty, and so many pasty-faced Turks squatting about in the filth grow tiresome. At first, they are described in letters home as fascinating and picturesque, and whole days are spent with them, buying hundreds of things that are destined to be left in hotel bureau drawers and gradually lost. The souvenirs we buy in the mouskie seem to melt away. The precious stones we bought there turn to glass, the slippers become pasteboard, the gilt things tarnish, and the brass work bends itself into old junk, and the mouskie is only a confused dream; so no wonder the old traveler is proud that he can find his way about in it. He had probably begun to think that there had never been such a place.

But Egypt is full of real things, and probably the most real thing is the English occupation. Egypt herself is the best proof of how necessary to her well-being this is. It is hard to tell just how unhappy the fellaheen were before the English came. The Egyptian is not the sort of man that complains. After centuries of oppression, he now accepts whatever form of government is offered in a browbeaten way, shuffles along after his donkey, and pays his tax for bringing a few bundles of clover across the bridge into Cairo without a murmur and, judging by his looks. I doubt if he would make much disturbance if he found, some morning, that the tax on his clover had been doubled. He feels like a very small depositor in a broken bank. England is the largest creditor, straightening things out for them both, and he is satisfied.

There never were so many cooks trying to spoil a broth. Before the Khedive receives a consul-general, the Sultan of Turkey must first approve of him, and it is said that the Sultan allows months to go by before he gives his consent, which is his Oriental way of showing his authority. But Egypt is geographically so important that, despite herself, she will be saved, and with England's help, she will someday pay her debts, and in centuries to come, the fellah may learn to hold his head up like the Nubian.

There is no fear of Egypt becoming dull and commonplace, for if the East and the West should ever fight, it must be for the possession of her canal; and many an unborn soldier's reputations will be made before the railroad that has started up the Nile's valley reaches Cape Town. The same land that offers death and prestige to the strong gives life to the weak, and the tired rich man on his dahabiyeh and the soldier on the transport go up the Nile side by side, and in most cases, they both find what they are in search of.

72

Shepheard's, in all probability, will forever remain a composite portrait of Europe and Asia, with Cairo as its frame. Time has made, and probably will continue to make, some slight alterations in Upper Egypt's appearance, but the locomotive's whistle will have difficulty breaking Karnak and Thebes's silence and calm. And the present indications are that Egypt will remain faithful to the Pharaohs of old. Until the judgment day, she will, in all probability (assisted by the Nile, who made her), continue to resist the attentions of modern nations quietly and patiently wait for that last day.

"The kingdom of heaven is within you; and whosoever shall know himself shall find it."

—Egyptian Proverb

www.ingramcontent.com/pod-product-compliance
Lightning Source LLC
Chambersburg PA
CBHW072120150726
47999CB00005B/2056